Can snakes really be charmed? What do Komodo dragons like to eat? How can you tell the difference between an alligator and a crocodile? What reptile has the deadliest venom?

Find out the answers to these questions and more in . . .

Magic Tree House®
Research Guide

SNAKES AND OTHER REPTILES

A nonfiction companion to
A Crazy Day with Cobras

It's Jack and Annie's very own guide to reptiles.
  Including:
• Gliding lizards
• Pit vipers
• Why birds are reptiles
• Sea turtles
And much more!

Here's what people are saying about the Magic Tree House® Research Guides:

Your Research Guides are a great addition to the Magic Tree House series! I have used Rain Forests *and* Space *as "read-alouds" during science units. Thank you for these!!*—Cheryl M., teacher

My eight-year-old son thinks your books are great— and I agree. I wish my high school students had read the Research Guides when they were his age. —John F., parent and teacher

And from the Magic Tree House® website:

My son loves the Research Guides about knights, pirates, and mummies. He has even asked for a note- book, which he takes with him to the museum for his research.—A parent

The Research Guides have been very helpful to us, as our daughter has an abundance of questions. Please come out with more. They help us help her find the answers to her questions!—An appreciative mom and dad

I love your books. I have a great library at home filled with your books and Research Guides. The [Knights and Castles] *Research Guide really helped me do a report on castles and knights!*—A young reader

Magic Tree House®
Research Guide

SNAKES AND OTHER REPTILES

A nonfiction companion to
A Crazy Day with Cobras

by Mary Pope Osborne
and Natalie Pope Boyce

illustrated by Sal Murdocca

SCHOLASTIC INC.
New York Toronto London Auckland
Sydney Mexico City New Delhi Hong Kong

ISBN 978-0-545-38440-7

Text copyright © 2011 by Mary Pope Osborne and Natalie Pope Boyce. Cover art and interior illustrations copyright © 2011 by Sal Murdocca. All rights reserved. Published by Scholastic Inc., 557 Broadway, New York, NY 10012, by arrangement with Random House Children's Books, a division of Random House, Inc. Magic Tree House is a registered trademark of Mary Pope Osborne; used under license. SCHOLASTIC and associated logos are trademarks and/or registered trademarks of Scholastic Inc.

12 11 10 9 8 7 6 5 4 3 2 1   11 12 13 14 15 16/0

Printed in the U.S.A.   40

First Scholastic printing, April 2011

*For everyone working to save sea turtles
and all other endangered animals*

Scientific Consultant:

CLYDE PEELING, Director, Clyde Peeling's Reptiland, Allenwood, Pennsylvania.

Education Consultant:

HEIDI JOHNSON, Earth Science and Paleontology, Lowell Junior High School, Bisbee, Arizona.

Very special thanks to the folks at Random House who help us so much: Gloria Cheng; Mallory Loehr; Chelsea Eberly, our excellent photo researcher; Sal Murdocca, our great artist; and as always, special thanks to our editor, Diane Landolf.

SNAKES AND OTHER REPTILES

Contents

Dear Readers,

Snakes! What do you think when you hear that word? Maybe you think, "Yikes, I'd better get out of here!" Snakes seem to scare a lot of people. We must admit that at first snakes seemed a little scary to us. There are several living near Frog Creek. We wanted to learn all about our snake neighbors and whether we should be afraid of them. We knew that snakes belong to a huge group of animals called reptiles.

To learn all we could about reptiles, we went online and then took a trip to the library to get books. We talked to our

teachers and read and read. We learned that reptiles come in all shapes, sizes, and colors. Some can be harmful to people, but most of them are not. In fact, reptiles do a lot of good for the planet. We learned so much that we feel great about snakes living near the tree house. So come on! Let's head for the rain forests, woods, and fields to get to know snakes and other reptiles.

Jack

Annie

1

Snakes and Other Reptiles

Reptiles have been on earth for millions of years. There are many thousands of kinds, or *species* (SPEE-sheez), of reptiles. They include snakes, *crocodilians*, lizards, turtles, and birds. Alligators, gharials, crocodiles, and caimans make up the crocodilian group.

Reptiles come in all shapes, colors, and sizes. Some, like saltwater crocodiles,

Saltwater crocs are the largest of all living reptiles.

can weigh over 2,000 pounds. Others, like dwarf gecko lizards, are less than an inch long.

There are reptiles on every continent. They live on land and in water. Some live in the steamy rain forests. Others live in deserts, in oceans, and in the treetops. There are even reptiles living in your backyard.

Modern reptiles are related to reptiles that lived millions of years ago. These included dinosaurs, snakes, crocodiles, and flying creatures as big as cars. Most early reptiles became extinct.

Many dinosaurs became extinct about 65 million years ago.

Those that survived slowly changed into the reptiles we know today. Even though they may not all look and behave alike, reptiles have many things in common.

Reptile Skin

Early reptiles, including dinosaurs, had scales. Like your fingernails, scales are made of *keratin*. They come in different patterns. The patterns are helpful in telling one species from another. All modern reptiles have some form of scales. Snakes, lizards, and crocodilians are covered in them. Turtles' shells are bony plates covered with scales called *scutes*. The ancient relatives of birds also had scales. Over thousands of years, some of the scales changed and became feathers.

This is a close-up of a python's scales.

Reptiles never stop growing. As they grow, they must shed their outer skin. This is called *molting*. Young reptiles molt six to seven times a year. Older animals may do so only once or twice a year. Crocodilians, turtles, and lizards shed in patches. Unless snakes are very large, they usually shed their skin in one piece.

Reptile Eggs

All reptiles come from eggs. Most reptile babies hatch from eggs laid by their mothers. But some lizards and snakes give birth to live young. Eggs develop in the mother's body, and the babies come out alive.

Except for crocodilians and birds, most reptiles don't care for their eggs. The sun warms them for several weeks until they hatch.

Cold-Blooded

All reptiles except birds are cold-blooded. This doesn't mean that their blood is cold. It means that they can't make their own body heat. They control their temperature by moving from sun to shade.

When it is very cold, reptiles go into a state of *brumation*, which is like hibernation. They curl up under rocks or brush and look as if they are asleep. Their body functions slow down, and they stop eating. Brumating reptiles use very little energy.

In spite of not eating during brumation, reptiles lose almost no weight.

If the temperature gets extremely hot, reptiles such as the desert tortoise burrow underground or find shelter away from the heat. They begin a process called *estivation*. As in brumation, body functions slow down, and the reptile remains passive until the weather gets cooler.

17

Vertebrates

All reptiles are *vertebrates*. People are also vertebrates. Vertebrates have skeletons with backbones. Backbones are made up of a series of small bones called *vertebrae*.

Snakes have more vertebrae than other animals. Some have as many as 500! Most people only have thirty-three.

Thanks to their many vertebrae, snakes are extremely flexible.

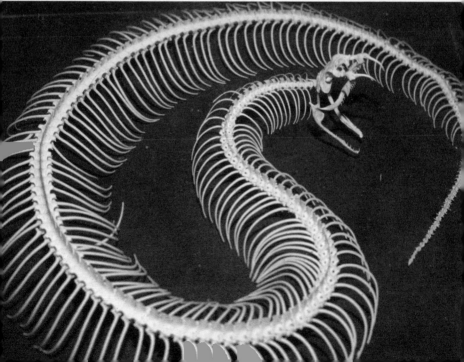

Harriet was a famous tortoise at a zoo in Australia who lived for over 150 years.

Great Old Age

Many reptiles live longer than other animals. Alligators and crocodiles sometimes survive for sixty or seventy years. Lizards can reach fifty. No reptile, however, can match the tortoise for old age. Some live over one hundred years.

The more we learn about reptiles, the more interesting they become. They are among the most diverse groups of animals in the world. Reptiles are also a great bridge to our prehistoric past.

19

Why Are Birds Reptiles?

This book focuses on cold-blooded reptiles. Birds are the only *warm-blooded* reptiles. The body temperature of warm-blooded animals stays the same in spite of the outside temperature. People are warm-blooded, too.

In the past, scientists didn't think of birds as reptiles. Recent fossil discoveries and new ways of classifying animals have changed their minds. Experts now group animals together if they have the same ancestors. Birds come from small bird-like dinosaurs. Some of these dinosaurs even had feathers and wings!

Because birds and other reptiles are related, they share certain things in common.

Some parts of a bird's skeleton are like those of the crocodilians. Birds have clawed feet like lizards, crocodilians, and turtles. They have scales on their legs and lay eggs. Scientists have found that birds are more closely related to crocodilians than to any other reptile.

2

Snakes

For thousands of years, people have both feared and respected snakes. Many believed they possessed magical powers. Some cultures created myths and legends about them. In ancient Greece, snakes were a symbol of healing and wisdom.

At times, snakes were even worshipped. In ancient Egypt, cobras were considered gods. There and elsewhere, people built temples to honor certain snakes. According to Hindu legend, the god Vishnu often rests on the coils of a giant cobra. Temples to snake gods still exist in India today. People often bring offerings of flowers and food for the snake gods.

Habitats

The place where an animal or plant lives is its *habitat*. Because they're cold-blooded, snakes don't have habitats in the Arctic or Antarctica. There are also no snakes in Ireland, Iceland, Greenland, and New Zealand. Otherwise, there are snakes all over the world.

Hey, wait a minute! There are no snakes native to Hawaii!

Snakes live in deserts, woods, fields, and rain forests. Green mambas and other snakes spend most of their lives in trees. Some of the largest snakes, such as anacondas and pythons, live near water deep in the rain forests.

Some snakes live in remote places. The rare Tibetan spring snake lives high in the mountains of Tibet near two hot springs. Sea snakes swim deep in the waters of the Pacific and Indian Oceans.

Snake Skin

When molting, snakes rub their noses over rough surfaces such as rocks or logs to loosen their skin. Except in very large snakes, the skin slips off in one piece like a glove. Many snakes are gray, olive green, and brown. Their dull colors blend into the background and protect them from predators.

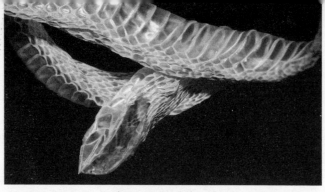

An eggeater snake shed this skin in one piece.

Some snakes' skins, such as the diamond python's, have beautiful patterns. There are also snakes with brilliant yellow, green, or red skins. The emerald tree boa in the rain forests of South America has a shimmering green skin that catches the light. Coral snakes in Florida and Arizona sport bright bands of red, black, and yellow or white.

Movement
Snakes use their muscles and the scales on their bellies to get around. Depending on the species and the surface, snakes move in

26

different ways. In the case of pythons, boas, and other heavy snakes, their muscles push their bodies forward. The scales on their bellies grip the ground and keep them moving ahead.

A few desert snakes, such as some rattlesnakes, slither across the smooth sand in a sideways motion called *sidewinding*.

Sidewinding snakes sometimes leave prints like these in the sand behind them.

Other snakes move in wave-like motions that begin at their heads and travel back to their tails. When climbing trees, snakes push their head forward and curl it around a branch. Then they pull the rest of their

In Indonesia, this paradise tree snake glides through the air from tree to tree.

body up behind them. Snakes cannot back up. Instead, they make a sort of U-turn.

At their fastest, most snakes move about three miles an hour. (You can run twice as fast.) Because they don't have legs, they move silently and can fit into very small openings.

Vision

Most snakes see movement well. If some-thing isn't moving, a snake will often ig-nore it. Snakes such as pythons, vipers, and boas have two pits near their nos-trils. The membranes in the pits detect heat from warm-blooded animals. This helps them hunt in the dark. They form an image of the animal they are tracking. Even when blindfolded, these snakes will still find their prey.

Snakes do not have eyelids.

Smell

Snakes smell with their tongues. They flick their forked tongue in and out of their mouth. The tongue picks up odor particles

The forks on a snake's tongue open wide to pick up the biggest range of scents.

from the ground and air. Snakes have something on the roof of their mouth called the *Jacobson's organ.* When their tongue touches it, messages go to their brain that tell them whether a good meal or danger is nearby. They know the direction of the smell by which tip of their tongue has the stronger scent.

Snakes are not the only animals with Jacobson's organs. Elephants, lions, and other reptiles have them, too.

Hearing

Snakes don't have outer ears. They "hear" by sensing the vibrations an animal makes when it moves across the ground. Sound waves travel from the ground to muscles and bones in the snakes' lower jaws. From there, the vibrations go to their inner ears and let them know that something is nearby.

Because snakes can't hear sounds in

the air, you can bang a drum, shoot a cannon, or sing "Yankee Doodle" and a snake won't hear you. But if you walk near where it's hiding, vibrations from your footsteps tell it that you are there.

When they get cold, snakes often lie on roads, where the asphalt is warm.

Staying Cool and Warm

Snakes control their temperature by moving from shade to sun. When it's cool, they lie in the sun. They often flatten their bodies or turn them toward the sun to get the most heat.

In order to stay cool, snakes seek shelter under rocks, trees, or brush. They sometimes go underground and cool down in rodent burrows or termite mounds.

Snakes brumate during cold winter months. They curl up under logs, rocks, and brush, often with other snakes. Then they go into a sleep-like state until spring comes.

Snake Babies

Some snakes, such as boas, water snakes, and rattlers, give birth to live young. Other snakes lay eggs, usually in the spring. Most leave the eggs on their own. The babies hatch about six or eight weeks later. Baby snakes have a special tooth called an *egg tooth* to crack their shells.

Unlike most snakes, pythons stay with their eggs. The females make a nest. Then they curl up around the eggs for about two months, until the babies hatch. Cobras also protect their eggs and remain nearby to guard them. The female king cobra pushes leaves and sticks together to make a nest. After she lays her eggs, she covers the nest in leaves and lies on top of it to keep her eggs warm. Scientists have recently learned that black-tailed rattlers remain with their young for about a week, until they first shed their skins.

These bushmaster babies are hatching in the rain forest of Costa Rica.

Food

All snakes are meat eaters. Small snakes eat rodents, lizards, birds, fish, eggs, and

When a snake swallows an egg, a projection under the vertebrae in the neck slits it open. The snake swallows the inside of the egg and throws up the folded shell.

insects. Larger snakes eat bigger animals such as deer, monkeys, sheep, pigs, and goats.

If your jaws were like a snake's, you could swallow a beach ball! Snakes swallow things that are much bigger than their heads. Their jaws open so wide that they swallow animals whole without chewing. Snakes don't have hinged jaws like people. Their jaws spread both sideways and downward.

A snake's skin is very elastic. As the snake "walks" its jaws around the prey, skin around its mouth stretches so the animal can slide down the snake's throat.

Predators
Pigs, birds, foxes, skunks, coyotes, and other animals eat snakes and their eggs.

 This crested serpent eagle has just caught a snake in its claws.

Eagles and hawks swoop down and grab snakes with their sharp claws.

Roadrunners are ground birds in the desert. They chase rattlesnakes and snatch them with their beaks. They kill them by

whapping them against the sand. Then they gobble the snakes up!

The biggest danger to snakes is humans. People often kill snakes, even harmless ones. They also destroy snakes' habitats and slaughter them for their skin. Snakes help keep the rodent population under control. They prey on rats and mice that carry diseases and eat crops. Some states have passed strict laws against killing certain kinds of snakes.

In parts of China, people eat snake soup.

Snake Charmers

Snake charmers often appear in the markets in India. They carry cloth-covered baskets of snakes slung across their shoulders. As a crowd gathers, the snake charmer sits down on the ground. Then he uncovers his baskets and begins to play a gourd flute.

Slowly, as if hypnotized, snakes rise from the baskets. They appear to sway in time with the music. If the snakes are cobras, they flare their necks as they stare intently at the snake charmer. Although the crowd might not know it, the snakes don't actually hear the music. They just follow the movements of the snake charmer. Snake charmers keep their snakes at a safe distance and are rarely bitten.

Snake charmers often come from families that have been in the business for hundreds of years. Today there are fewer snake charmers in the markets. New laws protecting snakes make it more difficult to own them. It's possible that snake charmers and their flutes will soon be a thing of the past.

3

Kinds of Snakes

Scientists group snakes into different *families*. Most snakes belong to the Colubridae family. Among these are garter snakes, racers, water snakes, and grass snakes. Although some Colubridae, such as the boomslang and the African twig snake, can be dangerous, most are harmless to people. Colubridae are on every continent but Antarctica.

One common snake in the Colubridae family is the colorful king snake. King snakes live throughout North America. They eat other snakes, including rattlesnakes and water moccasins. When threatened, they roll into a ball and play dead. They also give off a terrible smell that drives predators away.

Boas and Pythons

The longest land animals are in the Boidae and Pythonidae families. These snakes are also called boas and pythons. Boas and pythons have strong muscles that *constrict*, or squeeze, their prey. They coil around and squeeze their prey so hard that the heartbeat and breathing stop.

There are many smaller boas and pythons, some reaching only two or three feet.

Reticulated pythons in Southeast Asia are the longest snakes. They can reach over thirty feet. These snakes are excellent swimmers. They have been spotted out in the ocean far from land. Pythons live in Africa, Asia, Australia, and the state of Florida in the United States. Until people began bringing pythons into Florida as pets, they had never lived there before.

Anacondas, a kind of boa, are the biggest snakes if you consider how heavy they get. They can weigh 500 pounds and be over eighteen feet long! Anacondas are slow on land. In the water, they move quickly. Their diet consists of fish, goats, pigs, birds, sheep, and other animals. Once they've eaten, they can go for months without another meal.

After eating a duck, this brown water python is bulging.

Venom

Venom is the toxin that some kinds of snakes use to kill other animals. They inject it through their hollow fangs. These snakes are called *venomous*. Some snakes have several kinds of venom. One kind destroys the nervous system. Major body functions such as breathing fail and the animal dies. Other types of venom stop blood from clotting or damage tissues and cells.

North Carolina has the highest number of snakebites in the United States. Most are from copperheads.

India has the highest death rate from snakebites. Between 10,000 and 20,000 people die every year! Although there are about 8,000 venomous snakebites in the United States every year, fewer than ten people die from them.

Antivenin is a medicine for snakebites. To create it, small amounts of venom can be injected into animals such as goats or

46

A snake handler is <u>milking</u> this snake to
use its venom for making antivenin.

horses. The animals' blood builds up protection against the snake venom, which is extracted as antivenin.

Vipers

Almost all the venomous snakes in the United States are *vipers*. Vipers belong to the Viperidae family. Rattlers, water moccasins, and copperheads, as well as puff adders and the Gaboon vipers of Africa, are vipers.

Vipers have long, curved fangs in the

47

front of their upper jaws. When not in use, the fangs fold back and lie flat. As soon as the snake goes into action, the fangs swing forward. Ducts connecting two venom glands or sacs on either side of the snake's head carry venom to their fangs. When a snake bites down, venom is squeezed from the sacs into the hollow fangs and injected into its victim, just like a hypodermic needle.

Rattlesnakes make up a large portion of the viper family. There are about thirty different species. Rattlers get their name from the rattles on the tips of their tails. The rattles are made of loose, hardened segments of dead skin. When the snakes get nervous, their rattles may vibrate. The segments click against each other and make a whirring noise. Each time rattlers shed, they add a new segment to their rattle.

Rattlesnakes can strike over a foot away in a fraction of a second.

Elapids

Snakes in the Elapidae family are the most venomous of all. Elapids have shorter fangs than vipers. And unlike vipers, most have fangs that stay in place and can't fold back. Elapid venom attacks the nervous system. It is a superpowerful toxin that works quickly to paralyze the victim. It can cause death within a short time.

Elapids live mainly in Africa, South America, Australia and Asia. They include cobras, kraits, mambas, taipans, and death adders. The only elapids in the United States are two species of coral snake. Eastern coral snakes range from Florida north to the Carolinas and down to Texas. Arizona coral snakes live in Arizona, New Mexico, and parts of Mexico.

A group of cobras is called a quiver.

Deadly taipans and death adders live in Australia. The inland taipan has the most powerful venom of all snakes. They rarely come into contact with people. Because of this and effective antivenin, there are no recorded deaths from inland taipan bites.

Whether snakes are venomous or harmless, and whether they blend into the background or stand out with bright colors, they are unique and fascinating animals.

Come with us to meet some very unusual snakes!

King Cobra

King cobras live in India, China, the Philippines, and the Malay Peninsula. They are good swimmers and usually stay near swamps and rivers. They can grow up to fifteen feet long. One king cobra bite has enough venom to kill a cow or an elephant or twenty people!

A striking king cobra is an awesome sight. It lifts the front of its body three to six feet off the ground. Its neck flares out into a scary-looking hood. As the cobra moves toward its victim, it sounds like a growling dog. If an animal tries to escape up a tree, the cobra will go right up after it!

Black Mamba

Black mambas are the longest, fastest, deadliest snakes in Africa. These long, slender snakes account for many deaths. Black mambas are usually eight to twelve feet long. A single bite from a mamba has enough venom to kill fifteen to twenty-five people! In spite of their name, black mambas actually have gray skin. When they open their mouths, the inside is inky black (and scary!).

Black mambas try to avoid people. If cornered, they become very aggressive. Like cobras, they lift the front part of their bodies off the ground. They hiss, flatten their necks, and open their mouths very wide. When they strike, they do so numerous times at lightning speed!

Without black mamba antivenin, their

bite is often fatal. Many victims survive only about twenty minutes before paralysis or death occurs.

Eastern Hognose Snake

The eastern hognose snake gets its name from an upturned scale on the tip of its nose. It lives in the United States and parts of Canada. The hognose thrives in sandy soil. Its nose helps it dig burrows.

The hognose snake is harmless to humans. Its diet consists mostly of toads.

When attacked, a toad will puff up to defend itself. The hognose snake has sharp teeth it uses to deflate the unlucky toad.

Like the cobra, the hognose will hiss, rear up, and flatten its head to appear larger if threatened. It also strikes out at its predators. If all of this fails, the hognose puts on a second show. It will roll over, go limp, and play dead. Its mouth falls open and its tongue hangs out. Even though hognoses live in many places, they are rarely seen.

Mozambique Spitting Cobra

The Mozambique spitting cobra is native to Africa. Only the black mamba causes more deaths. This cobra is a small, slender snake that is olive gray. If threatened, it rears up, puffs out its neck, and sprays venom at the eyes of its attacker. The venom can hit something up to eight feet away! Spitting cobras have very good aim. If their spray hits an animal in the eyes, it can cause eye damage and even blindness.

Spitting cobras will bite if cornered. Their venom destroys the skin and tissue of their victims. Like the hognose, these snakes play dead and lie very still to fool their predators. Their diet consists of birds, eggs, insects, and small animals.

Eastern Coral Snake

These small, colorful snakes are related to cobras, mambas, and sea snakes. They have rings of red, black, and yellow or white around their bodies. The eastern coral snake is found mainly in the southern United States, especially in Florida.

Eastern coral snakes are rarely more than two feet long. They are nocturnal hunters that usually hunt in the early morning or late evening. Sometimes they appear after a hard rain.

Coral snakes are timid. When they are cornered, they curl their tails up tightly to show their dismay. Their short fangs deliver *very* toxic venom. It attacks the nerves and causes paralysis and death. Coral snakes have to hang on and chew their victim awhile to inject the most venom. These shy snakes rarely bite people. When they do, it's usually because someone has picked them up. There has been only one reported death from a bite since 1967, when coral snake antivenin was first produced.

4

Lizards

Lizards are closely related to snakes. Many experts say that snakes are actually a group of legless lizards. Lizards have more species than any other group of reptiles.

Lizards have moveable eyelids, long bodies and tails, short necks, and small heads. Like snakes, lizards come in all colors and sizes. The smallest is the jaragua (jah-RAH-gwah). It is less than an inch long and can fit on your fingertip!

The largest lizard is the Komodo dragon. These monitor lizards live on a few barren islands in Indonesia. Komodos can be over ten feet long. They are fierce animals with teeth like those of a *Tyrannosaurus rex*. They also have a deadly venom that causes their victims to bleed to death. Komodos actively hunt down other animals and have attacked and killed people.

Habitat

Lizards thrive in deserts, swamps, woods, and rain forests. Some, like marine *iguanas* (ih-GWAH-nuhz), spend much of their life in water. Many live high in treetops or in burrows.

Lizards brumate during cold weather. Desert lizards such as ground geckos and horned lizards sleep under the sand during the heat of the day. They hunt at night, when it's cooler.

Skin

Some lizards, such as chameleons, can change their skin color. They turn green, pink, blue, and yellow. They may do this for protection from predators, but it is

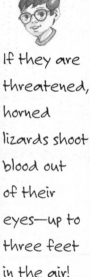

If they are threatened, horned lizards shoot blood out of their eyes—up to three feet in the air!

more often from fright or changes in temperature.

Getting Around

Most lizards have four legs. Many are great runners and climbers. The fastest land reptile is the six-lined race runner. It clocks in at eighteen miles an hour!

Basilisk lizards can run on two legs, even across water.

The common gliding lizard has skin on either side of its body that acts as sails as it glides through the air.

Geckos have invisible hairs on the bottom of their feet. These hairs help them cling to surfaces. Geckos can clamber up walls and race across ceilings.

Some lizards use their tail as an extra arm. Their tail grips branches as they scurry up trees. It helps them balance and move quickly. Other lizards' tails store fat. When food is scarce, the fat helps them survive.

Some lizards' tails break off if they are attacked. When a predator grabs the tail, it snaps off, allowing the lizard to make a quick escape. Some species have brightly colored tails. If they are threatened, they wiggle them in hopes that predators will attack their tails rather than their heads. If lizards lose their tails, some species will grow new ones while others will never have tails again.

Food

Different lizards eat different things. Many small lizards eat insects and worms. Marine

iguanas dive down underwater to feast on
sea algae growing on the wet rocks below.
Gila monsters eat small animals and insects.

Gila monsters, such as this one, have
venomous bites. So do Komodo dragons
and beaded lizards.

Spiny lizards are *omnivores* that eat both plants and animals.

Senses

Most lizards have good eyesight. They also have small outer ear openings that pick up sound. (Their hearing is better than a snake's.) The eardrums lie just under their skin.

Komodo dragons will also eat dead animals. They can smell them from miles away.

Like snakes, lizards use their tongues and Jacobson's organs to collect odors. Their sense of smell helps them find mates and identify predators and prey.

Certain chameleons have the longest tongue for their size of all animals. If you could touch something twelve feet away with your tongue, you'd be just like them. Their tongue flickers in and out with lightning speed. They can zap an

70

insect with its sticky tip in less than a heartbeat. When not in use, their tongues stay tucked up in the back of their mouths.

This Mediterranean chameleon catches a fly with its superlong tongue.

Lizards and Their Young

When lizards mate, the males work hard to attract females. Some display bright colors

 A male anole might stay puffed up like this for hours!

or inflate their throats. They bob their heads up and down. Sometimes they fight each other.

Species such as anoles have a *dewlap*, which is loose skin around their necks. Males puff up and nod their heads to attract females.

Some lizards make hissing sounds. Geckos are the only ones that make several types of sounds. When trying to attract females, males turn red and make tiny chirping, barking, and clicking noises.

Most lizards lay eggs. Others give birth to live young. And like most snakes, lizards don't stick around to care for their babies.

Night of the Iguanas

The winter of 2010 was a very cold one in the state of Florida. Iguanas and many other reptiles do not do well when it's below forty degrees.

One cold night, people thought they heard rain on their roofs. The next morning, they realized it was not rain at all. It was iguanas and other lizards falling out of the trees! The cold air had slowed down the lizards' body functions so much that they could not move. After the sun warmed them up, many of the lizards recovered.

One man thought the iguanas in his yard were dead. He piled them in his car to take them somewhere else and bury them. As they warmed up, the iguanas revived. Imagine the man's surprise to find his car full of very active iguanas!

Iguanas are native to South America and can't live in cold weather. They were brought to Florida by pet dealers. Many escaped or were set free. It's always a bad idea to remove animals from their natural habitats.

Reptile Smugglers

Reptile collectors will pay a lot of money for certain species. So smuggling live reptiles is big business. It can also be a risky business. Smuggling is against the law. If smugglers get caught, they may spend time in jail and pay big fines.

In 2009, a man trying to enter Norway from Denmark had fourteen harmless baby pythons stuffed into socks strapped to his chest. He also had ten albino gecko lizards in little boxes strapped to his legs. (And there was a tarantula in his suitcase!) Later the same year, officials in New Zealand stopped a German man trying to board a plane with forty-four lizards sewn into his underwear!

Smuggling reptiles is no joke. It harms them by taking them away from their natural habitats. It also harms other animals and their habitats when non-native animals escape or are released and breed.

5

Crocodilians

Crocodilians have been around for more than 240 million years. They have not changed much in 84 million years. Like their prehistoric ancestors, they have long tails, four legs, and scaly bodies. Their jaws are very strong and lined with jagged teeth. Crocodilians are closely related to dinosaurs and birds.

Crocodilians are often called crocs for short.

Crocodilians live in warm places. They are *semi-aquatic* animals that spend a lot of time in water. Crocodilians

79

thrive in swamps, rivers, lakes, ponds, and sometimes even the ocean. While swimming, crocs protect their eyes with extra

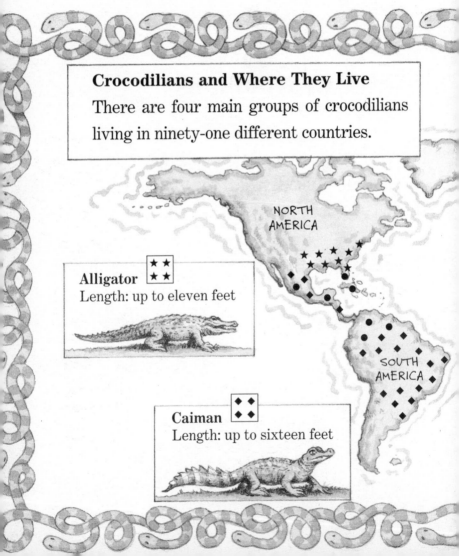

Crocodilians and Where They Live
There are four main groups of crocodilians living in ninety-one different countries.

NORTH AMERICA

SOUTH AMERICA

Alligator
Length: up to eleven feet

Caiman
Length: up to sixteen feet

transparent eyelids that act as goggles.
A flap closes their nostrils so that they
don't breathe in water. Like other reptiles,

Transparent
means see-
through.

Gharial
Length: up to twenty-one feet

ASIA

AFRICA

AUSTRALIA

Crocodile
Length: up to twenty feet

crocodilians have lungs. But they can stay underwater a long time without breathing—sometimes as long as an hour in cold water!

Crocodiles and gharials live in both salt and fresh water. They have special glands on their tongues to get rid of extra salt. Alligators and caimans do not have functional salt glands. They live more easily in fresh water.

Crocs swim by using their powerful tails. They sweep them from side to side like the rudder on a boat. Crocodilians also store fat in their tails. Because of this, they can go for a long time without food.

Saltwater crocodiles have been spotted 600 miles out to sea!

Finding Prey

Crocodilians hide in the water waiting for animals to come down to drink.

A floating croc looks a lot like a floating log.

Although crocodilians see well on land, their sight is not good in water. They find prey with sensory pits scattered around their jaws. These detect the smallest vibrations. Crocs also have a strong sense of smell.

High and Low Walkers

Crocodilians walk in two different ways. One way is called *high-walking*. When crocodilians high-walk, they hold their bodies

83

High-walking

up off the ground. They do so to avoid rocks and other obstacles. It is almost as if they are taking a stroll.

The other way they walk is called low-walking. When they low-walk, their bodies are close to the ground. They can move faster this way. They low-walk when running away or chasing something. For short distances, they can get up to ten miles an hour.

Low-walking

Teeth and Jaws

Crocs eat birds, bats, turtles, small deer, and other animals. Their sharp teeth clamp down tightly on their prey. Instead of chewing, they swallow in big chunks. Unlike other reptiles, crocodilians frequently lose and grow teeth. The new teeth come up in the hollows left by the older ones. In its lifetime, a crocodilian goes through as many as three thousand teeth.

When a croc bites down, its jaws are so strong and exert so much pressure that nothing can pry them open.

Gharials' jaws are so narrow that they can only eat fish.

Crocodilians are equipped with such powerful jaws, they can crush even the strongest turtle shells or bones with ease.

While they're sunning themselves, crocodilians open their mouths. This is called *gaping*. Experts think they might do this to release heat.

CROCODILES

Crocs' jaws are superstrong only when they bite <u>down</u>.

Right! If you put a rubber band around a small croc's jaw, it can't even open its mouth.

CROCODILES

Eggs and Babies

During mating season, male crocs make a lot of noise. They bellow and roar to attract females. After they mate, the females lay eggs in weeds, leaves, or holes.

Males sometimes fight over females by slamming their heads against their rivals.

87

These crocodile babies get a free ride on their mother's back.

Croc mothers guard the eggs until they hatch. This can take several months. When they're ready, the babies make squeaking noises. Like snakes, they use their egg tooth to crack the shell. Sometimes their mothers help by nibbling on the eggshells.

After the eggs hatch, croc mothers put the babies in their mouth. Then they take them gently down to the water. They watch over their young for a year or more.

Alligator or Crocodile?

People often confuse alligators and crocodiles. Alligators have rounder, shorter, and wider jaws than crocodiles. Their color is also darker. When crocodiles close their mouth, the fourth tooth on their lower jaw sticks out. This does not happen with alligators. The only place in the world where alligators and crocodiles live together is in the Florida Everglades.

Gustave the Legendary Croc

There are many tales of a killer croc that lives in the African country of Burundi. This croc is said to have killed as many as 300 people! The locals call him Gustave. They know him by a dark scar on his head. They claim Gustave is over twenty feet long and weighs about 2,000 pounds. Many experts say these stories are unlikely and that the number of killings is unbelievable.

People often fish, wash, bathe, and swim in the Rusizi River and Lake Tanganyika.

There are stories that Gustave travels between the river and the lake during mating season. People say he leaves a trail of half-eaten bodies behind.

No one has ever been able to capture Gustave or prove that the stories are true. Experts doubt Gustave could possibly have done all he's said to have done. Despite the lack of proof, Gustave is a legend that just won't go away.

6

Turtles and Tortoises

Turtles and tortoises appeared more than 200 million years ago. Fossils show that some were over ten feet long and weighed several tons! Today turtles and tortoises range from three inches to about eight feet.

Many turtles live in freshwater ponds, swamps, and lakes. Their webbed feet make them excellent swimmers. They only leave their watery homes to bask in the sun or lay their eggs.

Sea turtles spend most of their life at

sea. Females only leave when they lay their eggs on shore. Sea turtles have flippers and streamlined bodies made for swimming quickly. *Leatherbacks* are the largest sea turtles. Some weigh up to two thousand pounds and grow up to eight feet long!

Tortoises are large land turtles. Because they live on land, tortoises don't need webbed feet or flippers like other turtles. Instead, they have short, round legs for walking.

Their weight doesn't slow leatherbacks down. They swim over twenty miles an hour.

Shells

Turtle shells are part of their protective skeletons. In most turtles they are hard. The shells consist of about sixty bones covered by scutes. The bones are connected to their spine and ribs. Turtles can't just stroll away from their shells.

Experts can tell the age of a turtle by markings on its shell called growth rings.

94

They go together. Turtles never shed their shells. They grow right along with them.

Leatherback sea turtles have softer, lighter, and more flexible shells. They sometimes dive 3,000 feet underwater. If their shells were hard, the water pressure would crush them.

Some species, like the American box turtle, pull their heads, legs, and feet all the way inside their shells. Other species only hide parts of their heads and legs. Turtles known as side-necked turtles tuck their necks sideways along their shells to protect their heads and necks.

This side-necked turtle hides its head and neck between the edges of its shell.

Eggs on the Beach

Once a year, people see an amazing sight on beaches around the world. Hundreds of female sea turtles crawl up on shore on moonless nights. They use their flippers to dig holes in the sand and lay their eggs. Turtles return to the same beach where they were hatched. When they finish digging and laying their eggs, the turtles crawl slowly back into the sea. About fifty days later, the eggs hatch. Guided by light reflected from the water, the babies head straight for the ocean.

All turtles lay eggs. They usually bury them in the ground or in leaves and brush. Most female turtles leave the nests right after they lay their eggs. Turtle eggs are often at risk. Birds, skunks, and snakes eat them. People do as well.

Sea turtles can lay as many as 150 eggs at a time. Only a few survive.

Food

Many turtles are *omnivores*. This means they eat plants as well as insects and small animals. Snapping turtles gobble up water plants, birds, fish, snakes, and just about anything else they can find, including dead animals. They have very wide throats and swallow big hunks of food.

Some turtles, like green sea turtles and tortoises, are strictly vegetarian. Other sea turtles eat shrimp, crabs, fish, clams, and even jellyfish.

Galápagos tortoises eat a lot of plants. They have to. Some weigh over 500 pounds!

Snapping turtles have a very powerful bite. Don't ever touch one or pick one up!

Turtles see well, especially at night. They also have a good sense of touch and hearing. Snapping turtles and sea turtles actively hunt down their prey. Others wait for something to come their way. Turtles don't have teeth. Instead they have sharp beaks with very hard edges like a bird's. They use their beaks to cut and chew food.

Turtles and tortoises have survived for millions of years. They look very much like their prehistoric ancestors. But many turtles are now endangered, sea turtles especially. People hunt them for food. They also kill them to turn their shells into ornaments and use their skin for leather. Because people have cleared so much land for building, many turtles are in danger of losing their habitat. But many other people all over the world are working hard to make sure these ancient and fascinating animals stay around for a long time to come.

The North American wood turtle thumps its legs to make a sound like falling rain. This brings earthworms up to the surface.

Chinese Turtle Myths

The ancient Chinese often told myths and stories about turtles. They thought that turtles held the keys to wisdom, long life, and endurance. For centuries, the Chinese studied markings on turtle shells in hopes of predicting the future.

Chinese myths say that the whole world rests on the back of a turtle. In one myth, a ruler named Fu Xi is supposed to have discovered writing by examining turtles. He believed that all the markings of heaven and earth were on their shells.

In Taiwan today, people buy turtles made out of flour. They take them home hoping that the flour turtles will give them good luck for the coming year. The Chinese also believe that patting a turtle's shell will bring good fortune.

7

The Future of Reptiles

Have you ever heard of gator holes? During the dry season, alligators hollow out deep holes in the swamp. Even without rain, the holes stay full of water. Over the years, the alligators keep expanding their holes. Many animals could not survive without the water they find there.

Nature is like a chain with many different links. Each link is necessary for a healthy planet. For example, when turtles eat water plants, they keep lakes and ponds from being overgrown with weeds. When lizards eat mosquitoes and other bugs, they control the insect population. When snakes eat rats and mice, they protect farmers' crops. Reptiles are very important links in keeping the natural world in balance.

Reptiles and Science

Reptiles are also very important in the medical world. There are now drugs made from snake venom. Medicines for heart problems and high blood pressure come from the venom of a Brazilian snake. Chemicals in snake venom have also produced pain-killing drugs and creams. Now researchers say that substances in snake venom might slow down the growth of cancer.

Scientists also learn about the rate of

climate change by studying the reptile population. Even the smallest rise in temperature is harmful for many species.

Because turtles show few signs of aging, scientists are studying them to uncover the secrets of their long lives.

Saving Reptiles

Reptile habitats are constantly being polluted and destroyed. Illegal selling of reptiles is also taking a big toll on the reptile population. Today groups are working together to protect endangered reptile species. They are especially concerned about leatherback sea turtles and are working hard to help them survive. Groups across the United States rescue injured sea turtles. People all over the world are now acting to protect these wonderful creatures.

If you think about all the incredible reptiles that exist, saving them is a very important thing. Komodo dragons, Gila

monsters, chameleons, hognose snakes, leatherback sea turtles, and barking geckos all depend on good people just like you.

Doing More Research

There's a lot more you can learn about snakes and other reptiles. The fun of research is seeing how many different sources you can explore.

Books

Most libraries and bookstores have lots of books about reptiles.

Here are some things to remember when you're using books for research:

1. You don't have to read the whole book. Check the table of contents and the index to find the topics you're interested in.

2. Write down the name of the book. When you take notes, make sure you write

down the name of the book in your note-book so you can find it again.

3. Never copy exactly from a book.
When you learn something new from a book, put it in your own words.

4. Make sure the book is nonfiction.
Some books tell make-believe stories about reptiles. Make-believe stories are called *fiction*. They're fun to read, but not good for research.

Research books have facts and tell true stories. They are called *nonfiction*. A librarian or teacher can help you make sure the books you use for research are nonfiction.

Here are some good nonfiction books about snakes and other reptiles:

- *Amazing Snakes!* by Sarah L. Thomson

- *Reptile*, Eyewitness Books series, by Colin McCarthy

- *Reptiles*, National Audubon Society First Field Guide, by John L. Behler

- *Slither and Crawl: Eye to Eye with Reptiles* by Jim Arnosky

- *The Snake Scientist*, Scientists in the Field series, by Sy Montgomery

- *Snakes* by Seymour Simon

Museums and Zoos

Many museums and zoos have exhibits on snakes and other reptiles. These places can help you learn more about them.

When you go to a museum or zoo:

1. Be sure to take your notebook!
Write down anything that catches your interest. Draw pictures, too!

2. Ask questions.
There are almost always people at museums and zoos who can help you find what you're looking for.

3. Check the museum or zoo calendar.
Many museums and zoos have special events and activities just for kids!

Here are some zoos with reptile exhibits:

- Audubon Zoo, New Orleans, Louisiana

- Bronx Zoo, New York City, New York

- Cincinnati Zoo, Cincinnati, Ohio

- Clyde Peeling's Reptiland, Allenwood, Pennsylvania

- Houston Zoo, Houston, Texas

- National Zoo, Washington, D.C.

- Phoenix Zoo, Phoenix, Arizona

- Reptile Gardens, Rapid City, South Dakota

- Saint Louis Zoo, St. Louis, Missouri

- San Diego Zoo, San Diego, California

DVDs

There are some great nonfiction DVDs about snakes and other reptiles. As with books, make sure the DVDs you watch for research are nonfiction!

Check your library or video store for these and other nonfiction titles about reptiles:

- *King Cobra*
  from National Geographic

- *Nature: Reptiles: Snakes & Lizards*
  from PBS

- *Reptile*, Eyewitness DVD series,
  from DK Publishing

- *Super Snake*
  from National Geographic

The Internet

Many websites have lots of facts about snakes and other reptiles. Some also have games and activities that can help make learning about reptiles even more fun.

Ask your teacher or your parents to help you find more websites like these:

- animals.nationalgeographic.com/animals/reptiles

- enchantedlearning.com/subjects/reptiles/printouts.shtml

- 42explore.com/turtle.htm

- kidzone.ws/lw/snakes/facts.htm

- sandiegozoo.org/animalbytes/t-turtle.html

- www.vanaqua.org/education/aquafacts/
  crocodilians.html

- worldbook.com/wb/worldbook/
  cybercamp/html/walkturt.html

Good luck!

Index

Photographs courtesy of:

MARY POPE OSBORNE and NATALIE POPE BOYCE are sisters who grew up on army posts all over the world. Today, Mary lives in Connecticut. Natalie makes her home nearby in the Berkshire Hills of Massachusetts. Mary is the author of over fifty books for children. She and Natalie are currently working together on more Magic Tree House® nonfiction.

Here's what Natalie and Mary have to say about working on *Snakes and Other Reptiles*: "One day Natalie was hiking with some friends in the mountains in Arizona. Suddenly they heard the sound of rattling. After they quickly moved away from the trail, a beautiful little black-tailed rattlesnake peeked out of the leaves. Both of us have lived in places that have had venomous snakes. We were never afraid, because we realized that snakes just want to be left alone.

"Reptiles are everywhere. There are huge snapping turtles in the wetlands near our houses. One comes up every year and lays her eggs in the garden next door to Natalie's house. The turtle has done this for over twenty years! Many of us have a reptile story or two. Knowing all about these wonderful animals makes meeting them a lot more interesting."